A Message from God's Creatures

Written by Dorothy K. Ederer
Designed by Christopher W. Tremblay

Dedication

I dedicate this book to all animals lovers, especially:

Char and Mike Nickolson

John, Shannon, Kayleigh, Paige and Parker Murphy

Colleen, Rob, RJ and Jacob Galacz

Gerri and Joe Navarre

Gary and Sharon Riggi

Ann and Gary Hurleypalmer

David and Debbie Heiss

Randy and Donna Friedman

Carmen and Lyndon Cronen

Greg and Jeanne Causley

Acknowledgements

I am extremely grateful to Christopher Tremblay for
designing the interior and the
unique cover for this book.

Thank you to Gary Pearce for sharing his photographs
so they could be featured in this book.

I am also grateful to Sue King and Jessica Tomlinson
for editing this book.

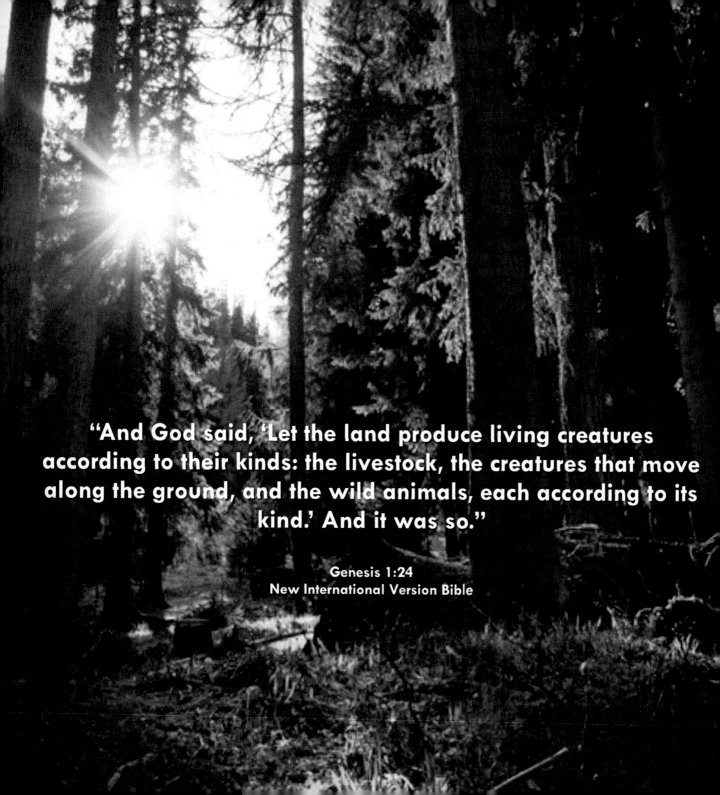

"And God said, 'Let the land produce living creatures according to their kinds: the livestock, the creatures that move along the ground, and the wild animals, each according to its kind.' And it was so."

Genesis 1:24
New International Version Bible

Welcome to God's country!

Get ready to meet some of the animals
God created for us.

SHEEP

FUN FACTS

A sheep's lifespan is 10-12 years. George Washington, Thomas Jefferson, and James Madison all raised sheep.
One pound of wool can make up to 10 miles of yarn.
A sheep, depending on the breed, can produce between two and 30 pounds of wool a year. It is estimated a sheep's field of vision is between 270 and 320 degrees. Sheep are not able to turn themselves over if they are on their back.

Luke 15:3-6

"Suppose one of you has a hundred sheep and loses one of them. Doesn't he leave the 99 in the open country and go after the lost sheep until he finds it? And when he finds it, he joyfully puts it on his shoulders and goes home. Then he calls his friends and neighbors together and says, 'Rejoice with me; I have found my lost sheep.'"

God, help us to be strong in our faith and willing to help those who are lost and struggling in life.

GIRAFFE

FUN FACTS

The giraffe is one of the gentlest and tallest animals. They are 20 feet high and are peaceful creatures who never attack unless threatened. Their skin patterns are like human fingerprints, no two are alike. A giraffe heart is huge, it is two feet long and weighs 20 pounds. Because of their long necks, giraffes can see things other animals cannot and will warn them of danger. A typical giraffe neck can stretch as long as six feet.

"And of every living thing of all flesh, two of every sort shalt thou bring into the ark, to keep them alive with thee; they shall be male and female."

Genesis 6:19

God, help us to have a big heart and be willing to stick our neck out for others who may be in harm's way.

HORSE

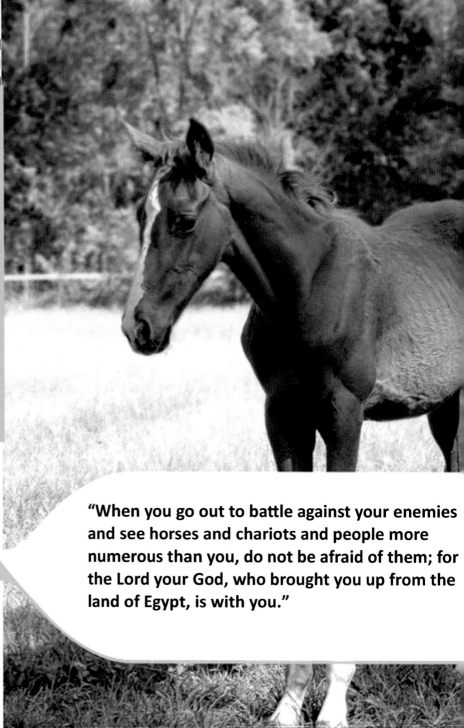

Deuteronomy 20:1

"When you go out to battle against your enemies and see horses and chariots and people more numerous than you, do not be afraid of them; for the Lord your God, who brought you up from the land of Egypt, is with you."

God, we always turn to You when we are fearful of what may happen to us when we wander away from You.

FISH

FUN FACTS

Fish have been on this earth more than 450 million years. There are over 25,000 identified species of fish. Forty percent of all fish occupy fresh water. Fish have a specialized sense organ called the lateral line, which works much like radar and helps them navigate in dark or murky water. Fish have excellent sight, touch, and taste and many possess a good sense of smell and hearing. Fish feel pain just like other mammals and birds.

"...While they were still in disbelief because of their joy and amazement, He asked them, 'Do you have anything here to eat?' So they gave Him a piece of broiled fish, and He took it and ate it in front of them..."

Luke 24:41-42

God, may we always be willing to share with others who are hungry and in need.

DONKEY

FUN FACTS

Donkeys have excellent memories. They can remember other donkeys they have met 25 years ago as well as a place they have been to. They never get involved in an activity if they believe it is unsafe. A donkey can live for more than 40 years. Donkeys by nature are herd animals. Their prefer to stay in groups, but a single donkey can actually live happily with a group of goats. Donkeys are considered to be all-terrain animals.

John 12:14-16

"Jesus found a young donkey and sat on it, as it is written: 'Do not be afraid, Daughter Zion; see, your king is coming, seated on a donkey's colt.'"

God, may we always be there for others when they need us and willing to give of ourselves.

ROOSTER

FUN FACTS

Roosters, adult male chickens, are the protectors. A rooster, at four months old starts crowing. Hens will lay eggs regardless of whether a rooster is around or not. A rooster's job is the fertilization of those eggs. A rooster will mate with all the hens in a flock. A rooster is symbolic of prosperity, honesty, protection, and good fortune. My niece has a rooster statue in her kitchen because it is supposed to bring you good luck.

"Before the rooster crows, you will have denied me three times."

Luke 22:24

God, we never want to deny You. You have always been there for us. Help us always to be faithful to You.

BEAR

FUN FACTS

Bears eat mostly fish and meat, but also like some plants, bulbs, and insects. Even though bears are big and heavy, they can run very fast and are good at swimming and climbing. They are one of the more intelligent mammals. Bears hibernate in the winter and their cubs are born in litters of one to three. Cubs stay with their mothers for about three years. Most bears live alone, except when a female has cubs.

Colossians 3:13

"Bear with one another and forgive whatever grievance you have against one another. Forgive as the Lord has forgiven you."

God, help us to forgive others and not hold any resentment in our heart.

EAGLE

FUN FACTS

Eagles are a powerful symbol of America. They usually mate for life. Eagles pair up at four or five years of age and live to be 38. Eagle nests are two to four feet deep and four to five feet wide. Eagles usually soar with their wings almost flat. We often hear the phrase, "eagle eyes," because they have sharper vision than people. Eagles can also see ultraviolet light.

"...but those who hope in the Lord
  will renew their strength.
They will soar on wings like eagles;
  they will run and not grow weary,
  they will walk and not be faint."

Isaiah 40:31

God, we are always running to something, help us to slow down and take time for You and not grow weary.

DOG

FUN FACTS

A female dog carries her puppies for 60 days before they are born. Adult dogs have 42 teeth. Their sense of smell is more than 1 million times stronger than human's, and their sense of hearing is more than 10 times more accurate than a human's. The average dog can run at full speed about 19 miles per hour. A dog's nose print is similar to a person's fingerprint. The only sweat glands a dog has are between its toes.

Luke 1:45-16

"But against any of the children of Israel shall not dog move his tongue, against man or beast: that you may know how that the Lord does put a difference between the Egyptians and Israel."

God, may we be open and accepting of those who are different and make them feel welcome in our community.

COW

"'Put a ring on his finger and sandals on his feet. Bring the fattened calf and kill it. Let's have a feast and celebrate. For this son of mine was dead and is alive again; he was lost and is found.' So they began to celebrate."

Luke 11:32

God, may we always rejoice when one who has been lost comes back to You.

PIG

FUN FACTS

A pig's pregnancy lasts 114 days. She can give birth to seven to twelve piglets two times a year. Pigs are intelligent animals and have an excellent sense of smell. They eat plants and animals. Pigs provide us with pork, bacon and ham. A pig has small lungs and 44 teeth. They have toes on each hoof, but only use half of them to walk. Pigs never have their toilet area anywhere near to where they eat or sleep.

Luke 11:16

"He longed to fill his stomach with the pods that the pigs were eating, but no one gave him anything."

God, we turn to You when we are hungry for love and in need of forgiveness.

LAMB

FUN FACTS

Young sheep are called lambs. They are vegetarian. Their field of vision is nearly 300 degrees, allowing them to see behind themselves without having to turn their heads. They like to stay close to others in a herd. A lamb's digestive system has four chambers, which breaks down what they eat. China has the largest number of lambs in the world.

"The wolf and the lamb will feed together, the lion shall eat straw like the ox; but the serpent—its food shall be dust."

Isaiah 65:25

God, help us to be open and accepting of those who are different. May our hearts draw others to live in peace.

LEOPARD

FUN FACTS

Leopards like to live alone. Females give birth to one or two cubs. They are born blind and start to see in 10 days. They live with their mother for two to four years. Mothers teach their cubs to climb, swim, hunt, and protect themselves from predators. They can leap up to 20 feet and are great swimmers and climbers. They run 36 miles per hour. Leopards weigh between 80-200 pounds. They hunt for food at night.

Isaiah 11:6-7

"The wolf will live with the lamb, and the leopard will lie down with the goat; the calf and young lion and fatling will be together, and a little child will lead them. The cow will graze with the bear, their young will lie down together, and the lion will eat straw like the ox."

God, we all desire to live in peace. May we never allow prejudice to enter into our heart.

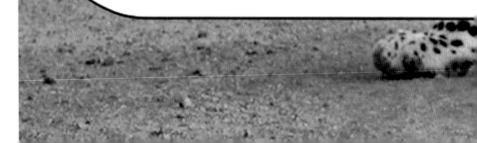

CAMEL

FUN FACTS

Camels can live for months off of the 80 pounds of fat that is stored in their humps. They can drink up to 40 gallons of water at one time. They can carry up to 900 pounds for 25 miles a day. They can run up to 40 miles per hour. Camels carry their calves for 14 months before giving birth. Camels have three sets of eyelids and two rows of eyelashes to keep sand out of their eyes. They can shut their nostrils during sandstorms.

"Again I tell you, it is easier for a camel to go through the eye of a needle than for someone who is rich to enter the kingdom of God."

Matthew 19:24

God, help us give generously without counting the cost. May people mean more to us than things.

FOX

FUN FACTS

Foxes can produce one litter per year, which is about one to 11 pups. They are born blind and open their eyes nine days after birth. They stay with their mother in the den while their father brings them food. They live with their parents until they are seven months old. Foxes have sensitive whiskers and spines on their tongues. They walk on their toes, which accounts for their elegant, cat-like tread. They are not pack animals.

Matthew 8:20

"Jesus replied, 'Foxes have dens and birds have nests, but the Son of Man has no place to lay his head.'"

God, may we always find a place not only in our hearts, but also in our homes for those who are lost or homeless.

DOVE

FUN FACTS

Doves and pigeons are often used interchangeably; however, doves have longer tails. They can live between 10 to 12 years. They may range in size from 15 to 75 centimeters. They can weigh about 4.4 pounds. Doves are the strongest flyers in the world because they have powerful wing muscles. They love to eat seeds and fruit. They drink a lot of water to help them digest the large amounts of seeds they eat.

"As soon as Jesus was baptized, he went up out of the water. At that moment heaven was opened, and he saw the Spirit of God descending like a dove and alighting on him. And a voice from heaven said, "This is my Son, whom I love; with him I am well pleased."

Matthew 3:16

God, we all long to hear that we are pleasing to You and living a good life.

HAWK

FUN FACTS

The lifespan of hawks is 10 to 20 years. They have excellent hearing and eyesight. They can see up to eight times more than the sharpest human eye. Hawks can fly 150 miles per hour. They use their sharp talons to catch prey both in the air and on the ground. They eat small mammals.

Job 39:26-28

"Does the hawk take flight by your wisdom and spread its wings toward the south?
Does the eagle soar at your command and build it nest on high?
It dwells on a cliff and stays there at night; a rocky crag is its stronghold."

God, may we continue to grow in wisdom and spread Your love wherever we go.

GOAT

The female goat has a gestation period of five months. Their pupils are rectangular and their vision is 320 to 340 degrees. The babies can stand and take their first steps within minutes of birth. A goat's milk is easier to digest than cow's milk. Their milk is higher in calcium and vitamin A. Goat meat is the most consumed meat worldwide. They are social animals, but not herd oriented.

"There will be enough goats' milk for your food, for the food of your household and maintenance for your girls."

Proverbs 27:27

God, may we always provide enough nourishment for our children. May no one ever starve in our world today.

DEER

FUN FACTS

A deer can walk a half hour after being born. A male deer is a 'stag' and a female deer a 'doe', while a baby deer is a 'fawn'. They can jump up to 10 feet and are very good swimmers.
A male deer will grow new antlers each year. A deer has 310-degrees vision because its eyes are on the side of its head [humans have 180-degree vision].

Psalm 42:72

"As the deer longs for streams of water, so my soul longs for you, my God."

God, our soul longs to be with You each day, no matter what we may encounter. Never let us wander away from You.

CRANE

FUN FACTS

Cranes usually lay two eggs. Two to four months after birth they get feathers. Some cranes will travel 500 miles in a day to get food. They have been clocked flying 45 miles an hour. They eat whatever they can find: fish, amphibians, small rodents, insects, berries, seeds and different plants. The average lifespan of the crane is 20-50 years. If there is any danger, the male and female come together to defend their territory.

"I chirp like a swallow or crane; I moan like a dove. My eyes grow weak as I look upward. O Lord, I am oppressed; be my security. What can I say? He has spoken to me, and He Himself has done this. I will walk slowly all my years because of the anguish of my soul..."

Isaiah 38:14-15

God, we turn to You when we are oppressed and feel secure in your presence. Stay with us on our spiritual journey.

TURTLEDOVE

FUN FACTS

The turtledove is an easy bird to identify. They weigh 4.2 ounces. Since the 1960's, their numbers have dropped. They migrate largely at night, covering up to 700km in one flight, and flying at speeds of around 38 miles an hour.

In *The Bible*, the "Song of Songs" refers to turtledoves mating for life. They have become cultural emblems of devoted love. The turtledove is one of the most abundant and wide-spread of all North American birds.

Luke 2:22-24

"When the time came for the purification rites required by the Law of Moses, Joseph and Mary took him to Jerusalem to present him to the Lord, and to offer a sacrifice in keeping with what is said in the Law of the Lord: 'a pair of turtledoves or two young pigeons.'"

God, at baptism we gave ourselves to You. May our lives be a reflection of our unconditional love for You.

FROG

FUN FACTS

Frogs are amphibians. They lay their eggs in water, which hatch into tadpoles. Tadpoles have gills, and their lungs grow when the tadpole matures into a frog. Frogs breathe water through their nose and absorb water into their skin, so they have no need to drink. A frog cannot survive if its skin dries out. They use their tongue to catch their prey. Frogs push their food down by retracting their eyeballs.

"Then the Lord said to Moses, "Go to Pharaoh and tell him that this is what the Lord says: 'Let My people go, so that they may worship Me. But if you refuse to let them go, I will plague your whole country with frogs.'"

Exodus 8: 1-2

God, may we allow others to be free so they can do what they feel called to do with their life.

GRASSHOPPER

FUN FACTS

A single grasshopper can eat half of its body weight in plants per day. There are around 11,000 known species of grasshoppers found around the world. They grow to around two to five inches. They can jump about 25 centimeters off the ground and cover one meter of distance. They are a very good source of protein. In the United States, grasshoppers cause about $1.5 billion in damage to grazing lands per year.

Leviticus 11: 21

"...However, you may eat the following kinds of winged creatures that walk on all fours: those having jointed legs above their feet for hopping on the ground any kind of locust, katydid, cricket, or grasshopper."

God, sometimes we hop from one thing to another. Help us to focus on one thing at a time.

OWL

FUN FACTS

There are 200 different owl species. Most owls hunt insects, small mammals, and other birds. Owls are active at night. They are farsighted, which means owls cannot see things close to their eyes. They have a flat face and large eyes, while barn owls have a heart-shaped face. An owl can turn its head nearly 270 degrees. They have powerful claws, which help them catch and kill prey. The color of their feathers helps it blend into its environment.

"There the owl will make her nest; she will lay and hatch her eggs and gather her brood under her shadow. Even there the birds of prey will gather, each with its mate..."

Isaiah 34:15

God, may we never forget to care for our children and protect them from any danger.

PEACOCK

FUN FACTS

The peacock's tail, with its 'thousand eyes,' is associated with the Archangel Michael and symbolic of omnipotence. The peacock has been claimed to be a symbol of humility and a symbol of resurrection: "When the peacock sheds his feathers, he grows more brilliant ones than those he lost." Only the males are called "peacocks," the females are called "peahens," and the babies are called "peachicks." The peacock's average lifespan is 20 years.

2 Chronicles 9:21

"For the king had ships which went to Tarshish with the servants of Huram; once every three years the ships of Tarshish came bringing gold and silver, ivory and apes and peacocks."

God, when we practice the gift of humility we then can rejoice when others do well.

WOLF

FUN FACTS

The female wolves' average weight is 60 to 80 pounds and males weigh 70 to 110 pounds. They have gray, black or white fur. Wolves are the largest members of the Canidae family. They are excellent hunters and it is said that they live in more places in the world than any other animal, with the exception of humans. Wolves live and hunt in packs, which range from two or as many as 20 wolves.

"Beware of false prophets, which come to you in sheep's clothing, but inwardly they are ravening wolves."

Matthew 7:15

God, help us be aware of those who try and deceive or trick us into doing things that are not good for us.

PELICAN

FUN FACTS

Female pelicans lay one to five eggs and they hatch in the order laid. The incubation period is 28 to 36 days. Pelicans feed their chicks up to 30 times a day for the first month. Their web feet help them to be strong swimmers. Their wingspan can range from 6.7 to 11.8 feet. It is the only bird with a pouch under its bill. Their pouch can hold up to three gallons of water. Pelicans eat fish, frogs, and lobsters. A pelican's life span is 10-25 years.

Zephaniah 2:14

"Flocks will lie down in her midst, All beasts which range in herds; Both the pelican and the hedgehog will lodge in the tops of her pillars; Birds will sing in the window, Desolation will be on the threshold; for He has laid bare the cedar work."

God, Jesus shed his blood to feed us like the pelican who gives of itself to feed its young. May we too be willing to feed the hungry.

STORK

FUN FACTS

There are 19 species of storks. Storks communicate with hissing noises since they are almost completely voiceless. They are large, long-legged, long-necked wading birds with long stout bills. At four years old, white storks generally begin breeding. Storks stretch out their necks and let their legs dangle behind them as they fly, mostly by soaring on warm currents. They live 30-40 years.

"And the stork, the heron after her kind, and the lapwing, and the bat."

Leviticus 11:19

God, may we soar gracefully through life as we help others to live their dream and become all that You have destined us to be.

Word Search

```
W  F  P  H  O  R  S  E  B  T  N  S  T  O  R  K  F  L
D  I  O  I  B  H  E  A  G  L  E  S  F  A  R  A  T  A
R  E  U  X  G  C  O  W  L  R  O  O  S  T  E  R  M  M
G  I  R  A  F  F  E  G  G  O  A  T  W  O  L  F  D  B
C  P  W  D  A  D  O  G  K  S  B  E  A  R  O  H  O  B
R  E  F  I  S  H  L  L  E  O  P  A  R  D  Z  A  N  J
A  A  K  D  P  E  L  I  C  A  N  X  C  V  G  W  K  I
N  C  S  E  H  O  S  H  E  E  P  B  B  J  E  K  E  I
E  O  X  E  Z  T  U  R  T  L  E  D  O  V  E  B  Y  G
H  C  P  R  J  O  G  R  A  S  S  H  O  P  P  E  R  P
K  K  F  R  O  G  Q  E  C  O  W  K  C  K  P  O  D  A
N  M  C  A  M  E  L  D  A  U  D  O  V  E  R  R  D  R
```

Find the following words in the puzzle.
Words are hidden → ↓ and ↘ .

BEAR	EAGLES	HORSE	SHEEP
CAMEL	FISH	LAMB	STORK
COW	FOX	LEOPARD	TURTLEDOVE
CRANE	FROG	OWL	WOLF
DEER	GIRAFFE	PEACOCK	
DOG	GOAT	PELICAN	
DONKEY	GRASSHOPPER	PIG	
DOVE	HAWK	ROOSTER	

Parent-Teacher Page

This page is for use by parents and teachers. Use these questions to create activities for your children or students.

1. Draw a picture of your favorite animal.

2. Describe the last animal you saw in person.

3. If you could be an animal, which one would you pick and why?

4. Which animals do you own as a pet?

5. How many of the animals in this book live near you?

6. Which animal are you most afraid of in this book and why?

Source of the Fun Facts

Giraffe	chabad.org/kids/noahsark/animal_cdo/aid/455445/Jewish/Giraffes.htm
Sheep	modernfarmer.com/2017/12/6-facts-sheep-might-not-know
Horse	thefactsite.com/2016/06/horse-facts.html
Rooster	countrysidenetwork.com/daily/poultry/chickens-101/12-fascinating-facts-about-rooster
Donkey	factslegend.org/30-interesting-donkey-facts
Eagle	mentalfloss.com/article/79468/14-bold-facts-about-bald-eagles
Bear	kidskonnect.com/animals/bear
Cow	mnn.com/earth-matters/animals/stories/20-things-you-didnt-know-about-cows
Dog	dogtime.com/puppies/1954
Lamb	sciencekids.co.nz/science facts/animals/sheep.html
Pig	raiseyourbrain.com/25-weird-animal-facts-pigs
Camel	spana.org/blog/13-fun-facts-about-camels
Leopard	kidsplayandcreate.com/fun-leopard-facts-for-kids
Dove	tonsoffacts.com/27-interesting-bizarre-facts-doves
Fish	petcoach.co/article/interesting-fish-facts
Fox	mentalfloss.com/article/59739/14-fascinating-facts-about-foxes
Goat	livelyrun.com/from-the-farmer/goat-fun-facts
Hawk	justfunfacts.com/interesting-facts-about-hawks
Crane	interestingfacts.tv/animal-facts/10-little-know-interesting-facts-about-cranes-bir
Deer	onekindplanet.org/animal/deer
Frog	itsybitsyfun.com/frog-facts-for-kids.htm
Grasshopper	sciencekids.co.nz/science facts/animals/grasshopper.htm

Owl	sciencekids.co.nz/science facts/animals/owl.html
Turtledove	livingwithbirds.com/tweetapedia/21-facts-on-turtle-dove
Wolf	factretriever.com/wolves-facts
Pelican	justfunfacts.com/interesting-facts-about-pelicans
Stork	justfunfacts.com/interesting-facts-about-storks
Peacock	nationalgeographic.com/animals/birds/group/peacocks

Bible Verses for Each Animal

Biblegateway.com

Photography Credits

Cover	Silhouettes of Giraffes purchased from Canva
Giraffe	Royalty Free Use from Canva
Sheep	Royalty Free Use from Canva
Horse	Young Horse Standing in Paddock, Queensland, Australia purchased from Canva
Rooster	By Gary Pearce
Donkey	Royalty Free Use from Canva
Eagle	Royalty Free Use from Canva
Bear	Royalty Free Use from Canva
Cow	Royalty Free Use from Canva
Dog	Royalty Free Use from Canva
Lamb	Royalty Free Use from Canva
Pig	Pigs purchased from Canva
Camel	Camel Near the Beach purchased from Canva
Leopard	Royalty Free Use from Canva
Dove	Royalty Free Use from Canva

Fish	By Gary Pearce
Fox	Royalty Free Use from Canva
Goat	Royalty Free Use from Canva
Hawk	By Gary Pearce
Crane	Royalty Free Use from Canva
Deer	By Gary Pearce
Frog	By Gary Pearce
Grasshopper	Royalty Free Use from Canva
Owl	By Gary Pearce
Turtledove	By Gary Pearce
Wolf	Royalty Free Use from Canva
Pelican	Royalty Free Use from Canva
Stork	Royalty Free Use from Canva
Peacock	Royalty Free Use from Canva

Dove and Monkey on next spread were used Royalty Free from Canva.

Animals Reading Books on next page were purchased from Canva.

Enjoy these other publications by Dorothy K. Ederer and Christopher W. Tremblay

Dorothy K. Ederer's Books

The Colors of the Spirit
A Golfer's Day with the Master
A Golfer's Prayer Book
The Spirit Whispers
Whispers from the Spirit
Children Whisper to God
Spirituality of a Quilter
Jesus the Master Quilter
Wisdom for Life's Journey
Spiritual Nourishment
Nourish Your Soul
Love Stories
Time with the Divine
Seasons of Love
52 Weeks of Inspiration
Dorothy and Dominic's Daily Devotional
Fetty's Philosophy

Children's Books

Lucy's Laptop
The Wonderful Weather of God
Musical Instruments Believe
Going Places in Life
Joshua for Kids
Reach for the Stars
Jesus' Alphabet

Mandala Journals

Follow Your Heart
Live Your Dream
Believe in Yourself
The Power of Mercy
The Gift of Hope
Praying the Psalms

Christopher W. Tremblay's Books

Walt's Pilgrimage
Walt's Pilgrimage, Jr.
Walt of the Day
The ABCs of Walt
Life is a Celebration

Author & Designer

Dorothy K. Ederer, O.P.

Dorothy, a Grand Rapids Dominican sister, is one of seven children from Saginaw, Michigan. Some of the positions she has held over the years include: Catholic Chaplain for Holy Cross Services, director of campus ministry at Michigan State University, campus minister at University of Michigan and Western Michigan University, co-director of the Joshua Foundation, director of the Campus Ministry School in Boston, a staff member at Chautauqua Institution in N.Y., and a junior high teacher. In addition, she created a card game called *Good News*, [St. Mary's Press 2008], and scripted a video, *Connecting with God*, [Oblate Media 2002]. She is the author of 17 books co-author of 14 books. Dorothy's favorite animal is the dove.

Christopher W. Tremblay, Ed.D.

A Michigan native, Christopher W. Tremblay is an only child with a creative mind. He has served in a variety of higher education administrative roles over the years at Western Michigan University, Gannon University, University of Michigan-Dearborn, University of Wisconsin-Superior, and Michigan State University. He currently serves as the Director of External Engagement for the Michigan College Access Network (MCAN) in Lansing, Michigan. He is the creator of *Getting In*, a card game to help students understand the college admissions process. He is the author of 4 books about Walt Disney and a co-author of 14 other books. Visit waltspilgrimage.com. Christopher's favorite animal is the monkey.

Made in the USA
Middletown, DE
23 September 2021